POCKET
FASHION EXPERT

Explore A World Of Fashion

Written by Catherine Saunders

Contents

What Is Fashion?

For Barbie and her friends, fashion is individual, it's fun, and it's creative.

Fashion is about wearing clothes that you love. It's about feeling good in your favorite colors, being inspired by the world around you, and wearing clothes that reflect who you are. Great fashion should help you to do all the things you love in comfort and style.

In this book, Barbie has so many amazing ideas and useful tips to share with you! Let Barbie help you find your own style and show you and your friends how to create fabulous outfits from the clothes you already have in your wardrobe.

Chapter 1

Creating An Outfit

Barbie likes her clothes to reflect her personality, her passions, and even her mood each day. Here are some ideas to help you get creative with colors, patterns, prints, and styles. Ready to have some fun with your wardrobe?

Which Color?

Sometimes, the hardest choice for Barbie is what color to wear. She often wears bright colors to match her mood or to help perk up a gray, rainy day.

BARBIE'S TOP TIP

Barbie likes to organize her clothes by color. It's easy to pick colorful outfits and her wardrobe looks like a rainbow!

Wearing bright yellow reminds Barbie of sunshine.

DID YOU KNOW?

In some countries, certain colors are considered lucky or special. In China red represents happiness and luck, while in the Netherlands orange is a royal color and worn by national sports teams and fans.

Barbie loves brightly colored shoes!

Patterns And Prints

Barbie and her friends love to experiment with cute prints and fun patterns. They look and feel so playful! You can wear patterns from head to toe, or mix some solid and patterned clothes.

The red lip print on this playsuit is bright and bold.

DID YOU KNOW?

Many patterns are inspired by nature and the world around us, from spirals on seashells to hexagonal honeycombs. Bubbles, clouds, waves, and ripples, as well as flowers and animals, all make great patterns.

Don't be afraid to mix different patterns!

BARBIE'S TOP TIP

If you don't usually wear patterns, you could start with a simple gingham (check) in your favorite colors.

Think Pink

Everyone knows that Barbie's favorite color is pink. Her friends love it, too. Wearing something pink makes them feel fabulous and ready for anything. Do you have a favorite shade of pink?

Even Barbie's balloons are pink!

Barbie wears pink sparkles for a party look.

Different fabrics and textures look great together.

You can wear pink from your head ...

DID YOU KNOW?

Fashion is always changing. In the early 20th century, pink was seen as a color just for boys! Now, anyone can wear any color they choose. From fantastic fuchsia to brilliant bubblegum, the fashion for pink won't fade!

... to your toes!

BARBIE'S TOP TIP

There's no such thing as too much pink! You can combine different shades of pink or dress from head to toe in one shade. Go for it!

White sunglasses and a lilac bag go well with shades of pink.

Black And White

Black and white go with every other color and they also look great together. This classic combination is always an elegant choice for any type of outfit.

This black and white checked pattern is known as houndstooth.

BARBIE'S TOP TIP

Wearing black and white is a simple way to create an elegant outfit. However, if you want you can also add a pop of color with a belt, bag, or necklace.

Black with white dots looks cute.

Black pants can look formal or casual.

DID YOU KNOW?

The fashion for wearing white wedding dresses was started by the British Queen Victoria in 1840. Before that, wedding dresses were worn in a variety of colors. Red was especially popular.

One Color Style

Wearing one color doesn't have to be boring! This outfit combines five different shades of green, as well as different types of fabric for a fresh and interesting look.

This long green coat would also look great with a formal outfit.

DID YOU KNOW?

Different colors are linked to different moods and ideas. Green is often used to represent calm, happy, or peaceful feelings. It is also associated with nature, health, and even luck.

Leggings are so comfortable.

BARBIE'S TOP TIP

How do you feel when you wear different colors? Wear colors to match your mood or to help change it.

Hello Color!

Barbie and her friends love to have fun with color. Different colors can transform your mood, and might put a smile on other people's faces, too. Which colors will you wear today?

Bright colors and bold patterns are a fun combination.

Wearing bright colors makes you stand out.

This bright t-shirt has a colorful yet calm pattern.

It can be fun to wear the same colors as your friends.

Blue is a cool and calm color that suits everyone.

You can match your accessories, too.

If it's a rainy day, let your outfit bring the sunshine!

BARBIE'S TOP TIP

Be bold with color. If you're feeling shy or nervous, wearing bright colors might even make you feel a little more confident.

Wear different shades and textures.

Wearing one color looks amazing! It doesn't have to be pink ...

Colorful shoes, sandals, or boots can transform an outfit.

Making A Match

When creating an outfit, Barbie thinks about how the different parts will look. Coordinating colors creates a calm effect and can look really stylish.

> The main outfit color is light pink with light gray details on the skirt.

DID YOU KNOW?

People's opinions about which colors match (or clash) is often linked to their position on a color wheel. Colors near each other on the wheel often work well together.

> This diamond pattern is known as an argyle pattern.

BARBIE'S TOP TIP

It can be really fun to coordinate outfits with your friends by wearing the same colors. Blue and pink look great together!

> The black shoes match the skirt and headband.

Color Clash

Sometimes strong or opposite colors can "clash," and many people don't wear them. However, Barbie and her friends make their own rules. They think that clashing colors can look great!

Red and purple are a classic color clash.

BARBIE'S TOP TIP

Wearing clashing colors, such as yellow and blue, in thin stripes can be a fun way to introduce clashing colors.

Having the same background pattern links the three strong colors.

DID YOU KNOW?

How we respond to color can be affected by our eyesight, culture, and life experiences. So you might have different ideas to your friends about which colors match and which clash.

Super Stripes

Stripes are such a versatile pattern; they can be thick, thin, vertical, horizontal, or even diagonal. They can make an outfit feel fun, sporty, or classically stylish.

This simple striped dress is stretchy and comfortable.

DID YOU KNOW?

Stripes are often linked to fishers and sailors. A blue and white undershirt was worn by the French Navy in the 19th century. In the 20th century, fashion designers such as Coco Chanel made this pattern, known as the Breton stripe, popular.

Pink and red are often seen as clashing colors.

BARBIE'S TOP TIP

Stripes look great for any occasion, from casual to formal. If Barbie can't decide what to wear, a striped top always works!

Hitting The Spot

Barbie and her friends love wearing spots. They can be tiny dots or large spots, evenly spaced or randomly placed, a single color or multicolored.

DID YOU KNOW?

Most fabrics today are made by machines, so it's easy to create incredible spot patterns. However, before machines, dots had to be printed or sewn on by hand. Imagine how long that would have taken!

Pink hair chalk washes out easily.

These spots are big, bright, and bold.

BARBIE'S TOP TIP

Even a simple spotted accessory can transform an outfit. Try a spotted bag or headband, and don't be afraid to mix patterns—even spots and stripes!

Silver pants complete this fun look.

Party Ready

Going to a party can be a chance to put on a special outfit, something you don't get to wear very often. Whatever you choose to wear, it should be something that makes you feel fabulous!

Don't forget a coat or jacket!

Solid colors or patterns, wear what feels good on you!

Gold shoes, accessories, and details make this party outfit shine.

BARBIE'S TOP TIP

Sometimes adding an accessory, such as earrings, can transform a regular outfit into a perfect party look.

These friends are all wearing the same color.

Helping friends choose a party outfit is really fun.

Sequins shimmer and shine for a classic party look.

This outfit mixes silver and gold for extra sparkle.

Lay out your whole outfit to make sure you're happy with it.

These pink earrings match the bag.

This skirt and shirt create a simple, elegant party outfit.

Winter Warmth

Barbie keeps out chilly winter weather with lots of warm layers. From her cozy earmuffs to her sturdy pink boots, she's stylishly wrapped up from head to toe.

Fluffy earmuffs

Thick silver jacket

Woolly scarf

DID YOU KNOW?

The coldest place on Earth is Antarctica, where the lowest temperature ever recorded was -128.6° F (-89.2° C)! Visitors need to wear lots of layers with a thick "freezer" suit on top in winter.

Fleece-lined pants for extra warmth

Waterproof boots

BARBIE'S TOP TIP

The weather might be cold and gray in winter, but Barbie always chooses bright and colorful clothes. And, of course, pink works for every season!

Spring Style

In spring, the weather can vary from sunshine to rain showers, sometimes even on the same day! Barbie and her friends will always feel just right in dresses, denim, and sneakers.

Delicate lace flower pattern on dress.

BARBIE'S TOP TIP

Show your love of nature by wearing spring colors such as green, yellow, pink, and lilac.

Flower prints are perfect for spring.

Jeans suit most seasons.

DID YOU KNOW?

Spring is a time of new beginnings as plants and flowers grow, some animals wake from hibernation, and lots of baby animals are born. It's also the perfect time for a clear out of your wardrobe!

Lilac socks add an extra pop of color.

Summer Vibes

In summer, Barbie and her friends keep cool in bright colors and tropical prints. They love to spend time outdoors—at the beach, in the park, or just chilling in the backyard.

> These tropical fruits look good enough to eat!

DID YOU KNOW?

On hot days, light colored clothes help you stay cool. Light colors reflect sunlight away from you, while darker colors absorb heat and make you feel hotter.

> Tropical flower and green leaf print.

> This shade of pink is so summery.

> Sneakers are great all year round.

BARBIE'S TOP TIP

In summer weather it's important to stay in the shade during the hottest parts of the day. You should also protect your skin regularly with sunscreen.

Fall Colors

Fall is famous for its gorgeous colors as the leaves turn red, orange, yellow, and brown. Barbie likes to reflect these colors in her autumn outfits.

Light brown jacket keeps out the fall chill.

BARBIE'S TOP TIP

Fall can be rainy, so Barbie always keeps her rain boots handy. You're never too old to splash in puddles!

This dark pink goes well with fall shades.

Darker, thicker denim is best for fall.

DID YOU KNOW?

In fall, the temperature usually starts to drop, but some days can be as warm and sunny as summer. Always check the weather forecast so you know what to wear!

Cool Coats

Coats keep you warm and dry, but your coat can also make a bold fashion statement. A colorful coat can brighten up a plain outfit, while a stylish jacket can finish off an elegant look.

Coats come in different lengths. This short jacket is ideal for spring.

Feel great in a warm duffle coat in your favorite color.

Duffle coats have special toggle fastenings.

Draping a jacket over your shoulders is very chic!

This black and white check looks very elegant.

A bright coat can make you feel fabulous!

Puffer jackets and coats are padded for warmth.

Barbie feels a bit like she's wearing a teddy bear!

Fake fur is warm and cozy, and so much fun to wear!

This longer coat is made from wool and is ideal for cooler weather.

Frills And Ruffles

Frills and ruffles can totally transform an outfit. You can have one big ruffle or lots of smaller ones that make a bold statement, or one or two small frills to add a little detail.

This big frill transforms the neckline and sleeves of this dress.

BARBIE'S TOP TIP

Barbie loves a frill detail on a short sleeve. It adds interest and is cool and comfortable in hot weather.

The frill is in the same color and fabric as the dress.

DID YOU KNOW?

Some animals have frills, too. When the Australian frilled lizard feels under threat, it opens a colorful skin frill around its head to scare off predators.

Sparkle And Shine

Everyone deserves a little sparkle and shine in their life! Barbie and her friends love to wear sparkly clothes and accessories, whatever the occasion.

Metallic shades, such as on these headphones, also look great.

DID YOU KNOW?

Sequins were invented in Ancient Egypt. Some gold sequin-like disks were found on clothes inside Tutankhamen's tomb, and are more than 3,000 years old!

This sequined jacket could also be worn with a skirt.

BARBIE'S TOP TIP

Don't save your sparkly clothes for parties. Wear a little sparkle whenever you can. A sparkly hair accessory will brighten up your outfit and your day.

Chapter 2

Fashion Inspiration

Everyone's idea of fashion is different. Barbie's outfit choices are often inspired by the world around her, the things she loves, and her hobbies. Come and take a look and then think about what inspires you and your fashion.

Nature Rules

Barbie cares very deeply about nature. She loves to show her connection with nature through her clothes, with leaf patterns, animal prints, fruity accessories, and even weather themes!

BARBIE'S TOP TIP

Nature prints can be bright, bold, and fun. From a butterfly pattern to a colorful leaf print, nature is always in fashion.

Big, bright green leaves look summery.

This belted fruit purse is adorable.

These sneakers add a zingy citrus touch!

DID YOU KNOW?

"Swishing" is when you swap clothes that you don't want or that don't suit you instead of buying new ones. Have a swishing party with your friends—it's very nature friendly!

Star Quality

Star prints always look out of this world! They can be stylish, magical, fun, or just super cute. You could wear one big star or lots of tiny ones.

> These simple black and white stars are very elegant.

DID YOU KNOW?

Stars are actually round. However, humans draw them with points because when we look up at the night sky, starlight seems to radiate outward in different directions.

BARBIE'S TOP TIP

If busy prints aren't your style, try simple patterns that only cover part of your clothing.

> This dress is light, cool, and comfortable.

> Pink goes with everything!

Flower Power

Most flowers bloom in spring and summer, so that's when Barbie wears flower-inspired outfits. Flowers are bright and beautiful and come in many shapes and colors.

Pink and red roses often represent love and happiness.

DID YOU KNOW?

Flowers are brightly colored to attract insects and other small animals to feed on their nectar. The visitors then spread the pollen to other plants so they can make seeds and grow new plants.

BARBIE'S TOP TIP

A head-to-toe flower pattern can feel a bit overwhelming, so pair it with plain items if you want a more understated look.

Sandals match the red roses.

Rainbow Style

It's always amazing when you spot a rainbow in the sky! Wearing rainbow colors and patterns makes Barbie and her friends feel positive and joyful. Rainbows often symbolize hope and unity.

This rainbow-striped dress is simply stunning.

DID YOU KNOW?

Rainbows appear when sunlight hits rain at just the right angle and bends, splitting into seven colors. The colors are always in the same order: red, orange, yellow, green, blue, indigo, and violet.

BARBIE'S TOP TIP

Real-life rainbows are striped, but you can wear rainbow colors in any pattern you like, from tie-dye to polka dots.

35

Be More Animal

Barbie's love of animals can often be seen in her fashion choices. Funky animal-inspired prints can transform a plain outfit into something quirky and stylish, while animal-themed patterns look fun and playful. Can you be more animal, too?

BARBIE'S TOP TIP

Wearing animal print can be empowering. When Barbie wears leopard print she feels brave and bold, like a leopard.

This leopard-print coat stands out from the plain black outfit.

DID YOU KNOW?

Leopards' spots are called "rosettes" because they are actually rose shaped. Leopards use their spot patterns to blend in with their surroundings so their prey can't see them.

This print is leopard inspired but with a bright color twist.

Pink animal print is Barbie's dream pattern!

This teddy bear is super cute.

BARBIE'S TOP TIP

Be inspired by your favorite animal! Whether you're a cat person or a dog fan, wearing a print of your favorite animal will always brighten your day.

Beach Dreams

You can wear beach-inspired fashion anywhere. Bright ocean blues and themes such as ice cream, sunglasses, or surfboards bring summer beach vibes to any outfit.

This summer outfit has a tropical beach theme.

Palm trees are also a popular beach theme.

BARBIE'S TOP TIP

Beach colors are bright and bold. Pair sunny yellows and ocean blues with your favorite shades to create a dazzling beachy look.

DID YOU KNOW?

Beach fashion often features a fun palm tree print. We associate palm trees with hot weather and sunshine because these trees grow in tropical climates with warm summers and mild winters.

Yellow flip-flops complement the dress.

Sports Style

Sportswear is designed to allow your body to move and stretch. It's so comfortable that you can wear it every day! You can go sports casual or add your own twists.

> This tank top is loose, light, and adds a dash of color.

DID YOU KNOW?

Many sports clothes are made from a material known as spandex or elastane. This clever fabric can stretch up to six times its size but still ping back to its original shape.

BARBIE'S TOP TIP

Leggings are great for yoga, but they're also perfect for everyday wear. They're stretchy and come in amazing patterns.

> These silver joggers make a bold fashion statement.

Add Accessories

Jewelry, bags, hats, belts, and sunglasses can transform a look, provide a finishing touch, or just add an extra fun detail. Accessories can be practical and useful, too.

An elegant bag and cool necklace add glamour.

Big earrings make a big statement!

Earrings can add some glamour to a casual outfit.

There are lots of styles and shapes of sunglasses.

Sunglasses protect your eyes and look cool, too.

Hats look great in strong colors.

Hats and scarves add color and keep you warm.

A simple gold bracelet and cute heart sunglasses complete this look.

A straw hat is a great summer look.

Summer hats protect your face and hair from the sun.

BARBIE'S TOP TIP

There are so many types of bags to choose from. Think about what you need to carry, and find one that will hold everything you need and suits your style.

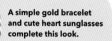

Camping Chic

Barbie and her friends love to spend time outdoors, especially camping out in the wilderness. Wearing clothes with a camping theme reminds them of these fun times wherever they are.

These trees also look like tents!

BARBIE'S TOP TIP

Camping clothes should be comfortable. Pack cotton t-shirts and stretchy leggings, plus a warm hoodie for when the sun goes down.

This colorful pattern is inspired by leaves.

Boots also look great with dresses.

DID YOU KNOW?

Outdoor activities such as camping and hiking can make you feel good. Fresh air and exercise decrease stress and increase the chemicals in your body that promote calm and happy feelings.

Nautical And Nice

Things that are inspired by the sea and sailing ships are known as "nautical." Nautical-themed outfits are always a fresh look. You certainly don't need to be anywhere near the sea to show off your nautical side.

> Blue and white are classic nautical colors.

DID YOU KNOW?

French sailors originally wore blue and white horizontal stripes so they would be easier to spot in the sea if they fell overboard and needed to be rescued!

> This boat print is charming.

BARBIE'S TOP TIP

Navy blue and white horizontal stripes are a classic nautical look. Other shades of blue and even other colors work, too.

> Red details contrast well with the blue and white.

Camouflage Print

Camouflage means using colors and patterns to blend into the background, but Barbie and her friends prefer to stand out in bright and fun "camo-" print outfits.

This modern camo print is colorful.

DID YOU KNOW?

Some animals use camouflage to hide; others use it to sneak up on their prey. Wearing camouflage-print clothes can be a great way to blend with nature and observe wildlife without being spotted.

This simple ruffle adds a fun detail.

BARBIE'S TOP TIP

Camo print is traditionally natural green and brown shades, but you can add any colors to give the camo look a modern twist.

White sneakers go with most outfits.

Check This Out

Check and plaid
(also known as
tartan) prints are so
versatile. They've been
around for centuries and
never go out of fashion.

This black and
yellow checked
dress is made from
soft brushed cotton.

BARBIE'S
TOP TIP

A soft wool or fleece
checked shirt is really
useful. Wear it with
jeans for a casual
outfit or with long
sleeves to protect your
arms when hiking.

Plaid shirt

DID
YOU KNOW?

Tartan prints are closely
linked to Scotland in the UK.
Many ancient families wore a
unique tartan design made
up of colored horizontal and
vertical striped patterns.

Classic sand-
colored boots

Denim Days

If you're not sure what to wear, you can never go wrong with denim. From jeans to shorts, dresses to overalls, denim works for every season, every style, and everyone!

A white t-shirt goes with everything.

Denim shorts are tough and practical for summer adventures.

The ruffle detail shows that denim can be glamorous.

Patchwork denim can look rustic and fun.

Denim softens the more you wear it.

This soft denim shirt is very versatile.

A denim jacket or shirt looks great over skirts or dresses.

DID YOU KNOW?

Jeans were created as durable and practical workwear for miners and factory workers. The first jeans were dark indigo blue. This color was chosen because it hides dirt and stains.

Jeans come in different styles and colors.

White denim jacket and black jeans.

"Double denim" is when you wear two different denim pieces.

Shorts And Sweet

Shorts are ideal for keeping cool in hot weather. They're great for creating many different looks, from sporty and casual to formal and sophisticated.

Cute cat eye sunglasses

DID YOU KNOW?

Culottes are long shorts that look like skirts! They became popular for women at a time when pants were mostly worn by men. Culottes gave women the freedom of wearing pants while still looking like they were wearing skirts.

You can match your shorts and t-shirt for a coordinated look!

Simple black cycling shorts can be dressed up or down.

Checked shirt, in case the weather gets cooler.

BARBIE'S TOP TIP

Denim shorts are great for summer. Barbie loves to wear them with a t-shirt or tank.

Let's Do Dungarees

Overalls (sometimes called dungarees) used to be worn to protect clothing, but Barbie and her friends wear them because they're comfortable, and practical—ideal for active days out with friends.

Overalls are pants with a bib and shoulder straps.

BARBIE'S TOP TIP

Denim overalls are super durable and practical. In summer, you can wear short overalls.

DID YOU KNOW?

Dungarees got their name from an Indian cloth called *dungri*, which was thick and durable. The first ones were worn by farm workers and later by female factory workers.

This spotted pattern is so fun.

Rolled up hems look fashionable.

Cool Customizing

Barbie and her friends love to be creative and have fun with fashion. Customizing clothing by adding extra details is a great way to create something unique, wonderful, and totally you.

BARBIE'S TOP TIP

Plan your customization carefully and make sure to practice the techniques to achieve the effect you want.

Some patches can be ironed on, with adult help.

DID YOU KNOW?

Many famous fashion designers started out by customizing and creating their own clothes. Coco Chanel learned to sew as a child, which helped her future career.

Fabric pens are great for adding details to clothing.

Lovely Layers

Layering pieces on top of each other looks great and is practical, too. Some days the weather can be hot, cold, rainy, and sunny, so a layered outfit makes you ready for anything.

> These silver details on the sleeves add a touch of sparkle.

DID YOU KNOW?

Layering can be very useful for sports and outdoor activities. Base layers are often made from special materials that are designed to keep you warm and dry.

> The shirt peeks out above and below the sweater.

> These pants are super soft.

BARBIE'S TOP TIP

Start with the thinnest layers so that the warmest, thickest layers are on top and can be taken off when you get too hot.

Fairy-Tale Fashion

Sometimes it's great to let your imagination run free. Put on an outfit that makes you look and feel like royalty, even if it's just to do your homework or hang out with your friends!

Wearing a tiara always feels great!

This outfit is fit for royalty.

DID YOU KNOW?

Fairy tales such as Cinderella are hundreds of years old. Different versions of the stories exist all around the world, and were shared by being spoken out loud before they were written down.

This rainbow dress is magical.

BARBIE'S TOP TIP

If you don't want to go full princess, just wear a tiara, a top with some sparkle, or a dazzling accessory.

Let's Dress Up!

Costume parties are super fun, and a great chance to experiment with your style. You can be anything you like! What would your dream costume be?

> Making your own fairy wings is fun.

BARBIE'S TOP TIP

Plan your outfits with your friends so you can coordinate your looks and help each other get ready.

> This skirt could also be worn with an everyday outfit.

DID YOU KNOW?

Legends of fairies exist all over the world. These magical beings are usually depicted as tiny humans with wings. They can be kind, helpful, mischievous, or powerful.

> This outfit is shades of pink and purple.

Fabulous Feet

What you wear on your feet is very important. Shoes, boots, sneakers, or sandals cushion your feet against the hard ground and protect them from sharp objects, dirt, and all sorts of yucky things. They can look great, too, of course!

These long boots are inspired by horse-riding boots.

Boots are usually warmer and sturdier than shoes.

Bright shoes can add color and fun to a plain outfit.

Boots go with everything, from skirts to pants.

Sneakers are best for a busy, active day.

Choose the right footwear for your day.

Sneakers are comfortable and flexible, so they're ideal for sports.

Leather is strong and goes with everything.

Sandals help keep feet cool in hot weather.

Only wear shoes that fit your feet well.

Glittery shoes look great for a party.

Chapter 3

Sports And Hobbies

Barbie has lots of fun hobbies, and what she wears for them is really important. Come and find out what she wears to help her move freely and confidently, feel good, or be part of a team.

Yoga Practice

Barbie and her friends love to do yoga together. It's all about moving and stretching gently, and focusing on breathing and relaxation. Stretchy, comfortable clothes are ideal for yoga.

Wear close-fitting clothes; loose clothes might get in the way.

DID YOU KNOW?

Yoga has been around for thousands of years, and is thought to have originated in India. Some religions incorporate yoga, but anyone can practice it just for exercise and relaxation.

Colorful cropped leggings

This position is called tree pose.

BARBIE'S TOP TIP

Yoga is good for your mind and body, so wear colors and patterns that make you feel calm and positive.

Horse Riding

Horse riding combines Barbie's love of the outdoors with her passion for animals. What she wears when riding must protect her body if she falls and also be comfortable to ride in.

A riding hat is essential for safety.

A vest keeps Barbie warm but allows her arms to move feely.

BARBIE'S TOP TIP

Riding pants, such as jodhpurs or breeches, protect your legs from bumps and also from rubbing against the saddle.

DID YOU KNOW?

There are many different horse riding events including show jumping, dressage, and racing, with each requiring a special outfit. Or you can just ride for fun!

A small heel on the boot helps keep the foot in the stirrup.

59

Time For Tennis

Tennis is a fun way to hang out with friends. Barbie loves to play doubles–two vs. two. A tennis match involves a lot of running, bending, and stretching, so flexible clothing is important.

This stretchy fabric also helps Barbie stay cool.

DID YOU KNOW?

A tennis racquet has strings that help control the direction and power of the ball. Tennis balls are made from felt and rubber for just the right amount of bounce.

This tennis dress comes with shorts underneath.

BARBIE'S TOP TIP

If you don't have a specific tennis outfit, any stretchy shorts and tank top or t-shirt would be suitable.

Soccer Player

Soccer is a popular sport because you can play it anywhere, from the beach to a backyard—all you need is a ball. Barbie plays for a team, so she wears the team's colors.

Every player has a different number on their shirt.

Shorts are usually a solid color.

BARBIE'S TOP TIP

You can wear any comfortable clothing for soccer. You can even wear your favorite pro team's uniform.

DID YOU KNOW?

In many countries women were not allowed to play soccer professionally for many years. Nowadays, there are professional women's leagues all over the world and youth teams for girls and boys.

Cleats have studs on the bottom.

Shin pads protect Barbie's legs.

61

Bags Of Fun

There are many types of bag, so you need to think about how you will use yours, what you need to fit in it, and even how you like to wear it. Here are some of Barbie and her friends' favorite bags.

A bag made from durable, waterproof leather will be long-lasting.

A backpack-style bag is big enough to hold a water bottle.

Wear your bag however you feel most comfortable!

This style of bag can be worn across the body or like a belt.

This style is inspired by a doctor's bag.

A vibrant pattern stands out against a plain outfit.

Quilted bags are a classic look. This one is big enough to fit a book in.

This bag is versatile, practical, and cute!

A bag like this can be worn on the shoulder, across the body, or carried by hand.

Baking Inspiration

You don't need special clothes to bake, although it's best to wear an apron in case of spills. This sweet cupcake t-shirt always inspires Barbie to create something extra delicious!

DID YOU KNOW?

A cupcake is not the same as a muffin. Cupcakes usually have frosting or icing on top but muffins don't. Muffins have all of their flavor in the batter, and can be made to taste savory or sweet.

Barbie hopes her cupcakes look as good as these!

BARBIE'S TOP TIP

A simple apron to wear when you're baking is a great project for a new sewer. With practice, you will be able to make all kinds of clothes.

Platform sneakers help Barbie reach utensils from the top shelf!

Skateboarder

When Barbie goes skateboarding with her friends their style is practical and comfortable. Long sleeves cover their arms, while pants and knee pads protect their legs when they fall.

> This helmet is for protection, but it also matches her shirt.

DID YOU KNOW?

Jeans started out as work clothes, but from about the 1950s they became a popular fashion item as well. Jeggings are a 21st-century invention that look like jeans but have the stretch and comfort of leggings.

BARBIE'S TOP TIP

A plaid shirt looks great worn over a t-shirt. It can be tied around the waist when you're not skateboarding.

> Stretchy jeggings help her flip and spin freely.

> Bright purple skateboard

Gymnastics

Hair is worn in a secure bun.

Gymnastics takes balance, agility, strength, and coordination. Exercises include leaps, spins, flips, and jumps, so gymnastics clothes must move and stretch with the body.

The high neck looks elegant and won't slip.

DID YOU KNOW?

Gymnastics started in ancient Greece, where physical fitness was considered to be a very important part of daily life. At that time, gymnastics included a wider range of exercises, from running to swimming.

A small frill adds a fun detail to the leotard.

BARBIE'S TOP TIP

Tight, stretchy clothes are best for gymnastics. Leggings, leotards, shorts, and t-shirts are all perfect because they move with the body.

Gymnastics is usually done barefoot.

Softball Uniform

Barbie enjoys playing team sports with her friends, and softball is one of her favorites. She loves it so much that she's designed her own softball uniform. Go, team Barbie!

Protective helmet

Team t-shirt with logo.

DID YOU KNOW?

The aim of softball is to score runs by batting a ball and then running around four bases. Some players wear special gloves to help them catch the ball (which is hard!) and stop the other team from scoring.

Special studded shoes help prevent players slipping.

BARBIE'S TOP TIP

For practice games, you don't need a uniform. Just wear comfortable sports clothes.

Group Style

Barbie and her friends like to dress in similar styles, but always make sure they show off their individual personalities and fashion sense. They also love to share fashion ideas and suggest outfits for each other.

Every outfit features classic black.

These party looks are all individually fabulous.

A short jacket looks great with pants.

Keeping it casual but stylish is the theme for this group.

Barbie and her friends always support each other when they try out new styles.

Each outfit has bright and bold colors.

These friends are all wearing statement colors.

Barbie is wearing a pale shade of her signature pink

BARBIE'S TOP TIP

It's fun to swap clothes with your friends, if you can. It's a great way to try out new looks or feel like you have a whole new outfit.

This group looks coordinated in summery prints and pastels.

Everyone thinks this hat looks fabulous!

Basketball

Many sports favor close-fitting or stretchy clothing, but basketball is the opposite. Long, baggy shorts and loose tanks allow free movement and also help cool air flow around the body.

DID YOU KNOW?

When basketball became popular for women in the late 19th century, players wore long skirts. Nowadays, women wear shorts that can be long and baggy or shorter and close fitting depending on their personal or team style.

Every player has their own number.

These basketball shorts are knee length and baggy.

BARBIE'S TOP TIP

You can wear a basketball jersey even if you're not playing a game. Sportswear makes great casual wear!

Comfortable sneakers are a must-have for basketball.

Ice Skating

Short, stretchy dresses or leotards are usually worn for ice-skating performances or competitions. However, ice skates are the only essential item for this sport.

DID YOU KNOW?

Several sports feature ice skates, from figure skating and ice dancing to ice hockey and speed skating. Each one requires a slightly different type of ice skate.

Skirts or leggings allow skaters to jump and spin.

Skaters usually wear tights to keep warm.

BARBIE'S TOP TIP

Ice rinks are cold! Wrap up warm with several layers when you go to practice or hang out with friends.

White skates are often worn for competitions.

Skiing

Goggles protect eyes.

Skiing outfits need to be warm but also flexible enough to allow the body to move and turn easily. Stretchy fabrics are ideal for skiing, and it's also a good idea to wear layers to stay warm in the snow.

BARBIE'S TOP TIP

Bright ski outfits look great and also help your friends spot you against the white snow!

Padded jackets are great for skiing.

These leggings are fleece-lined for extra warmth.

DID YOU KNOW?

Ancient skis discovered in Russia are thought to be up to 10,000 years old. At that time, skis would have been used for hunting and traveling around on snow-covered land rather than sports.

Special ski boots slot into the skis.

Swimming

When regular clothes get wet, they get heavy and stretch out of shape, so swimwear needs to be light and hold its shape when wet. Synthetic fabrics such as nylon, polyester, and elastane are best for this.

Goggles help Barbie see underwater.

DID YOU KNOW?

Before polyester, nylon, and elastane were invented, swimwear was made from natural materials such as wool. These would stretch and turn baggy when they got wet.

Barbie is a swimming champion.

A stretchy swimsuit helps Barbie move through the water easily.

BARBIE'S TOP TIP

Try to find out how your clothes are made. Some clever designers recycle plastic bottles and fishing nets to make their stretchy swimsuit fabrics.

Painting

Barbie doesn't need special clothes for painting—quite the opposite. She wears clothes that she doesn't worry about splattering paint on. When Barbie paints, it's going to get messy!

DID YOU KNOW?

There are lots of different styles of painting. Realistic paintings are usually what you see) while abstract styles use colors, patterns, and shapes to portray the world. What's your painting style?

BARBIE'S TOP TIP

An old pair of overalls can be very comfortable for painting, and the pockets are useful, too!

This skirt will look good with even more colors!

Any paint will wipe off these sneakers.

Dancing

Dancing is a great way to exercise and to have fun, and there are many types of dance to try. Barbie and her friends enjoy learning routines together and putting on shows.

Hair is loose and free.

BARBIE'S TOP TIP

Stretchy leggings and tops are best for dancing, so your body can move any way you want it to.

Two different-colored tops create stylish layers.

Cropped leggings

DID YOU KNOW?

Dancing isn't just for humans! Bees do a kind of "waggle" dance to show other bees where to find food. Other animals, such as Andean flamingos, dance to attract mates.

Bare feet are best for many dance styles.

Flexible Fashion

Barbie's favorite pieces of clothing are things that she can wear in lots of different ways, for different occasions, and even in different seasons. Take a look at some of her most versatile pieces. What's your favorite outfit?

Barbie also loves to share clothes with her friends.

This soft woolen top goes with skirts or pants.

This mid-length coat looks great with skirts or pants.

Here, the coat is draped over a spring outfit.

Clever layering can take a summer item into fall so Barbie can wear a favorite dress more often.

This yellow-gold dress is cool and light for summer.

Add a simple white turtleneck and tights for fall.

This blue skirt can be dressed up for a party or kept casual for everyday wear. How would you wear it?

BARBIE'S TOP TIP

Be creative with your clothes and think about how you can combine them in different ways. Don't be afraid to take fashion risks!

This floaty skirt suits everyone.

You can't go wrong with leopard print! This coat can be casual or formal and paired with fall, winter, or spring outfits.

Barbie is all wrapped up for winter!

What To Wear?

Sometimes it can be hard to pick out an outfit. Don't worry, Barbie is here to help! Try this fun quiz to help you decide what to wear. Whatever you choose will be fabulous!

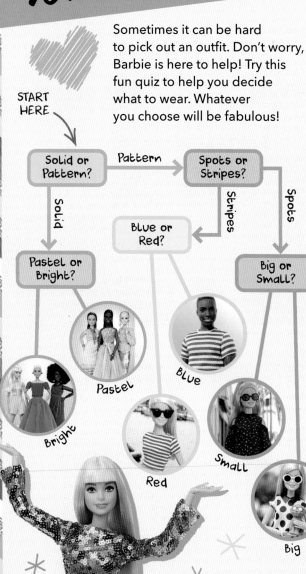

START HERE

Solid or Pattern?

Pattern → Spots or Stripes?

Solid

Stripes

Spots

Blue or Red?

Pastel or Bright?

Big or Small?

Blue

Pastel

Bright

Small

Red

Big

Glossary

Accessories
Extras added to decorate an outfit, such as jewelry, or a belt, a scarf, a hat, or a bag.

Camouflage print
This pattern is traditionally natural tones such as green and brown and is designed to help people blend in with nature or their surroundings.

Customize
To make clothing personal by adding unique details.

Elegant
Simple or classic in style.

Faux fur
Synthetic material that looks like animal fur.

Jeggings
Pants that look like jeans but are stretchy like leggings.

Jodhpurs
Pants worn for horse riding. They have extra material on the inside of the leg to protect riders.

Pastel colors
Pale, light, or soft colors.

Swishing
Swapping clothes with friends, often at a special party.

Tartan
A pattern associated with Scotland, made up of different colored horizontal and vertical stripes crisscrossing each other. Also called plaid.

Tie-dye
A twisty, swirly pattern that's achieved by tying the fabric so parts of it don't take up any color when dyed.

Trend
Something that is popular at a certain time.

Written by **Catherine Saunders**
Project Editor **Lisa Stock**
Senior US Editor **Megan Douglass**
Designer **Anne Sharples**
Project Art Editor **David McDonald**
Production Editor **Siu Yin Chan**
Senior Production Controller **Lloyd Robertson**
Managing Editor **Paula Regan**
Managing Art Editor **Jo Connor**
Managing Director **Mark Searle**

First American Edition, 2024
Published in the United States by DK Publishing
1745 Broadway, 20th Floor, New York, NY 10019

A catalog record for this book
is available from the Library of Congress.
ISBN: 978-0-5938-4046-7

Printed and bound in China

The publisher would like to thank
Bianca Hezekiah for providing
the authenticity read.

www.dk.com

www.mattel.com